Author

To my sunshine Amélie and to all fun secrets born and raised in Spanish class.

A mi pequeña Amélie y a todos los secretos divertidos que nacieron y crecieron en la clase de español.

Illustrator

To all the wonderful women that always surround me.

A todas las maravillosas mujeres que siempre me rodean.

Lil' LIBROS
www.LilLibros.com

Carlota Shares Her Secret / Carlota cuenta su secreto

Published by Little Libros, LLC

Text © 2021 Maria Rosana Mestre
Art © 2021 Ana C. Esparza
Book Design by Angie Vasquez

ISBN 978-1-947971-57-8

Library of Congress Control Number 2021935777

Printed in China

First Edition, 2021

26 25 24 23 22 21   5 4 3 2 1

CARLOTA SHARES HER SECRET

CARLOTA CUENTA SU SECRETO

Lil' LIBROS

Carlota almost fell over in laughter in her room
when she remembered her old secret. It was amazing,
the funniest fact someone could ever imagine.

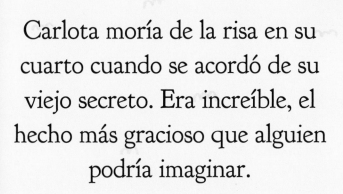

Carlota moría de la risa en su cuarto cuando se acordó de su viejo secreto. Era increíble, el hecho más gracioso que alguien podría imaginar.

She had to tell someone, someone that she knew wouldn't be able to resist telling a secret! She found her brother Luis in the hallway and told him the secret.
"When I was an ant, I thought that..."

¡Tenía que contárselo a alguien, a alguien a quien no resistiría contar un secreto! Encontró a su hermano Luis en el pasillo y le contó el secreto.
«Cuando yo era hormiga, pensaba que...»

And they laughed together.

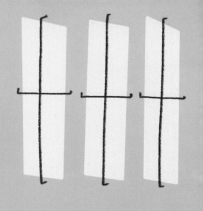

Y se rieron juntos.

Unable to keep the secret for more than ten minutes, Luis ran to Ernesto, the neighbor, and told him. "Carlota turned into a caterpillar and went to a dance contest."

Sin aguantarse ni diez minutos, Luis fue corriendo donde Ernesto, el vecino, y le contó. «Carlota se convirtió en oruga y fue a un concurso de baile».

At dinner, Ernesto opened the family conversation by sharing the secret.

En la cena, Ernesto comenzó la conversación familiar con el secreto.

The very next morning,
Ernesto's dad told Arnoldo,
his best work buddy, the secret.
"Then, when she was a dragonfly,
she dressed up like a rock star."

La mañana siguiente,
el papá de Ernesto le contó el
secreto a Arnoldo, su mejor
amigo del trabajo. «Entonces,
cuando era una libélula, se vestía
como estrella de rock».

Arnoldo arrived home for dinner.
He wanted to tell them the secret.
But he kept it.

Arnoldo llegó a su casa para la cena. Quería contarles el secreto. Pero lo guardó.

That same night, Carlota
waited for the arrival of their guests:
Ernesto and his parents.

Esa misma noche, Carlota
esperó la llegada de los invitados:
Ernesto y sus papás.

When the two families were together for a friendly coffee, the secret was revealed by its author.

Y al estar las dos familias reunidas para un café amistoso, el secreto fue revelado por su autora.

"When I was a little girl, I thought there were singing ants inside of the radio."

«Cuando era chiquita, creía que en la radio habían hormigas cantantes».

MARÍA ROSANA MESTRE believes imagination should be protected and defended in all children. Born in Venezuela, she is a reader, writer, and sworn translator; teaches Spanish as a foreign language to grandmas and grandpas, kids, and adults; and runs a building company with her husband. María Rosana received an MD in Literature from the Universidade Federal do Paraná (Brazil), a postgraduate degree in Creative Communication from Universidad Autónoma de Barcelona (Spain), and a BA in Print Journalism from the Universidad Rafael Belloso Chacín (Venezuela). She is the author of Trato Feito (Brazil, 2012). María Rosana believes in democratic values; for this reason, she is exiled from her country, which is under a dictatorial regime. She lives in Indiana with her daughter Amélie, her husband, her mom, and a little puppy named Río.

ANA C. ESPARZA is an illustrator based in Guadalajara, Mexico. Born in Sinaloa, she studied integral design and has always loved learning through the creative processes and people around her. The work Ana enjoys most is editorial illustration with educational and recreational purposes for all ages.